My Inner Strength

Tina Morgan

WestBow
PRESS
A DIVISION OF THOMAS NELSON

WestBow Press books may be ordered through booksellers or by contacting:

WestBow Press
A Division of Thomas Nelson
1663 Liberty Drive
Bloomington, IN 47403
www.westbowpress.com
1 (866) 928-1240

ISBN: 978-1-4908-0960-1 (sc)
ISBN: 978-1-4908-0961-8 (e)

Library of Congress Control Number: 2013917296

Printed in the United States of America.

WestBow Press rev. date: 09/27/2013

Acknowledgement

I honor my Lord and Savior, Jesus Christ for His power and might. For I walk in the dominion He has given unto me. In everything I give thanks. I am so grateful and I shall praise His name forever. Lord I love you.

To my husband Randy, I love you and thank God for you. Thank you for your love and support and believing in me.

To my children, family and friends I thank you for your love and support and believing in me. I could not have done this without God giving me you. I love you.

> *"I had fainted, <u>unless</u> I had believed to see the goodness of the LORD in the land of living. Wait on the LORD, <u>be of</u> good courage, and <u>he shall</u> strengthen thine heart; <u>wait</u> I say on the LORD."*
>
> Psalms 27:13-14 (KJV)

Foreword

This book of scripture, thought, prayer and declaration was written to help anyone who is in search of God in the inward parts. By hiding the Word of God in the heart and making application every waking moment will radiate the inner strength God has given to us all. Therefore if His words are in us then every need will be supplied because it is in the inner man for strength to pull from daily.

"Thy word have I hid in my heart that I might not sin against thee."
Psalms 119:11 (KJV)

This is also a book of study. Therefore, I beg of you to get an understanding of what God is requiring of us. This way we will walk hand in hand with the man that stills the waters and calms the seas in our lives. God bless you.

"Wisdom is the principle thing; therefore get wisdom; and with all thy getting get understanding."
Proverbs 4:7(KJV)

Table of Contents

An Extra Ordinary Love

The search for love has placed us into some cracks and crevices we choose to forget. But a closer look at our search reveals that we can't eliminate sin from our journey. All the love we thought was love turned out to still have us longing for a touch. A touch that would give us a satisfaction to where we would want no another kind of loves in its place, because we would be content. For Christ to love us so and think about us so long ago before we were even here; says that he went through some lengths to reach us. Now, that is some kind of love. Think, *while I was yet sinning . . . , Christ died for me. What a wonder, what a gift, what a magnificent thing was happening before I knew it!*

This is not an ordinary love, but an extra ordinary love that would reach through to us in time. A love that shows patience and kindness, sitting back and letting us have a go at what we think is life and love. A higher extra ordinary love that lifts us up from where we are and places us on a sure plateau above all confusion that has been offered to us as love.

Prayer

Father thank you for your son Jesus and the extra ordinary love you both have given. My heart is rich and filled with a real love I never knew. Allow me Lord to use this love to love my neighbor as I love you and myself. Amen.

Declaration

I declare with the love that Jesus has displayed for me. I will love because I am loved.

Scriptures of God's love

John 3:16, I Timothy 1:15, John 15:13

Prayer/thoughts:

Love Conquers

~*~

"If thine enemy be hungry, give him bread to eat; and if he be thirsty, give him water to drink; for thou shalt heap coals of fire upon his head, and the LORD shall reward thee."

Proverbs 25:21-22

~*~

Our first reactions to when some of us have been done wrong we immediately go into retaliation mode against that person or persons. Nor, do we stop to think what caused this wrong in the first place. Do we ever turn the situation inward towards us and do a self check? What we find is a back and forth battle that continues with no forgiveness, no compassion, and no understanding.

If we do turn inward towards ourselves then something like this may occur from the inside of us: *What did I actually say? What did I actually do to merit this action towards me? How can I better this situation? How can I change me?* Holding grudges is not the key here. In us we need to think about *what if I fall on hard times? Will I be harsh then and so puffed up in pride or would it merits me to be humble? If God is love and he loved me and gave to me and I am in his likeness and in his image; should I not give even to my enemy who at this time is in need?* God is so much more! To use the resources God has given to bless even an enemy; shows the love of Christ and an enemy may become a friend.

3

Prayer

God of the whole earth, you are an abundant provider in everything I could ever want. Make me to know thy love and show thy love even unto me worst enemy. For I know great is the reward for those that can love in spite of any evil doing. I thank you for teaching me love in a way I have never known how to operate in when I am being tried and tested. In Jesus name. Amen

Declaration

I declare by the wisdom of God that I will conquer by showing no retaliation, but the love that has been shown to me in my times of being an enemy to God that all might be provided for in love.

Scriptures to help conquer in love

II Chronicles 20:15, Luke 6:35-38, Luke 6:27-28, Matthew 5:43-45

Prayer/thoughts:

A Promise Coming Out Of the Familiar

~*~

"Now the LORD had said unto Abram. Get thee out of thy country, and from thy kindred, and from thy father's house, unto a land that I will shew thee: And I will make of thee a great nation, and I will bless thee, and make thy name great; and thou shalt be a blessing: And I will bless them that bless thee and curse him that curseth thee; and in thee shall all the families of the earth be blessed."

Genesis 12:1-3 (KJV)

~*~

lthough this scriptures points to Abram before he was named of the Lord to be called Abraham; there were some things Abram had to do. The first thing was hearken unto the voice of the Lord, secondly, get to stepping. This was not of his choice for direction but by the direction of the Lord. Then Abram would receive the blessing. Important that we see this journey unfold, and what God says next for this act of obedience. He will bless those that bless Abram and curse those that curse Abram. Traveling takes some preparation but we never know what will befall us in our travels. We can't take what we know on a journey with God. In other words our family traditions and methods we use for protection and provision. This is a new and living way. We must wait for instruction and direction if we intend to have a blessing and a name for Him in the earth. This means we become a stranger to whatever elements we move into. We will find welcomes and extra items added as we sit to rest and eat. We even find warnings to help keep us out of harm's way. The flip side is that we too must become a blessing and not a curse to the strangers we will happen upon or vice versa. For we are on a mission from the Lord to get to a place He will show. Obedience in its true form happens to us on this journey. Trust happens to us on this journey. For, we will no longer be the old man and his ways.

Prayer

Father God in the name of Jesus who makes all provision for me please lead and guide me to where you want me to be. Help me to trust and obey your voice. Cause me to know no stranger that I might be for you a blessing and not a curse. Amen.

Declaration

I declare that I will get to the place for which God intends for me. I will obey and trust his word as I move from my familiar to the unknown; knowing that He holds my blessing and my promise.

Scriptures

Matthew 25:37-40, I Samuel 15:22, Proverbs 3:5-6

Prayer/thoughts:

My Joyful Cry

"I will love thee, O LORD, my strength. <u>The LORD</u> is my rock, and my fortress, and my deliverer; my God, my strength, in whom I will trust; my buckler, and the horn of my salvation, and my high tower."

Psalm 18:1-2

Knowing God is the one thing that helps in the press of life we often get misinformed about. We speak of him or about him in such an unaffectionate way that instead of God being personal; most often there is a disconnection in the relationship and we never fully get all that he is to us. There is a joy that should instantly fall on us as we lift our voices up to cry unto God knowing he hears us and provision is there and we want for nothing.

The number eight which brings for us a new beginning can be associated with after God rested on the seventh day of creation the way we know it; he put into place the following day, (the 8th day) eight things he is to us that believe and trust in him: 1) God is a rock, 2) God is a Fortress, 3) God is a deliverer, 4) God is almighty, 5) God is strength, 6) God is a buckler/shield/defender, 7) God is the horn (power) of salvation, 8) God is a High tower(a place out of harm's way).

There shall be a loud cry of joy when a <u>believer says</u> they know him!

Prayer

Lord Jesus, thank you for hearing me when I cry and call upon your name. You are a friend to me indeed in the time of need. I know you hear and you answer in just the right time. Glory to your name forever! Amen

Declaration

I declare that my cry will be joyful in knowing I can talk to God Almighty who hears me at every hand. I declare that as the days go by I will get to know him even more.

Scriptures

Psalm 116, II Timothy 2:15, Psalm 46:10, Psalm 34:17

Prayer/thoughts:

When Word Hits My Ears

"And thine ears shall hear a word behind thee, saying, This is the way, walk ye in it, when ye turn to the right hand, and when ye turn to the left. Ye shall defile also the covering of thy graven images of silver, and the ornament of thy molten images of gold; thou shalt cast them away as a menstruous cloth; thou shalt say unto it, Get thee hence."

Isaiah 30:21-22 (KJV)

Turning away from the things that held us bound at a time of our ignorance soon fades away as we hear softly but firmly in our ears a word that comes from the Lord. When the word hits the ears something churns within us and we find ourselves letting the filth and the attention getters go. We no longer want to be caught up and entangled with sin once we have heard a word from the Lord that says to get away from the unclean thing and separate you. This means there is a blessing coming and the blessing is something that happens when a word hits the ear that manifests from the inner parts of us to move toward God and as we move towards Him we see the things that held us bound more clearly and we dare not turn to either side to go back. Our eyes open because of the words that hit our ears. Our hands become lifted in praise and worship because a word hit our ears. Our heads become bowed and our knees bent because our ears have heard a word that has gone down into the depths of us and sprung up life that no idol no matter how shiny it appears can shine brighter than that word which hit our ears. It is an inward, outward move happening from God and nothing fake can take the place of the word that hits the ears.

Prayer

Most Holy and all wise God, speak a word that I may grow and live and have my being in you. Your word is life and I thank you for speaking life into me. For causing me through your word to see the idols I had placed between me and thee. Now Lord speak forever more that I will cast off and cast out all things I have put before you that I may have what you have for me. In Jesus name I pray, Amen.

Declaration

I declare to stay before the Lord that I may hear a word for him that has made me. I declare that idol or image I have put before me to worship, I will cast down and out! In Jesus name

Scriptures

Zechariah 13:1-2, Colossians 2:21-23, Galatians 4:1-3, Hebrews 5:12

Prayer/thoughts:

Blessings and Violence

"Blessings are upon the head of the just: but violence covereth the mouth of the wicked."

Proverb 10:6

When violence is in a person, there is no telling what he will say or do to puff him higher than what he actually is. In turn one does not realize that God sees and knows all and when your intentions are not right a dark end follows you. We should not speak of ourselves as to show confidence in our abilities. They all belong to God. Where is the faith and confidence in trusting in God for all to come into manifestation before all?

Blessings are in abundance to those that walk by faith, live by faith, speak by faith and work by faith. A just man will have praise unto the Lord and He will give him what is needed for success. If a man follows Christ who is just in every aspect, then one can say to live by Christ and is to say the just shall live by faith. This is one that believes God for every jot and speck of faith for existence with this trying journey of justice.

Prayer

Jesus, let every part of me be a blessing to you. I want to be just and right. I need your help so that I will be a blessing and not a curse. I desire to be humble and true. Amen

Declaration

I declare that I will walk by faith in Christ Jesus and the words that I speak will be right and pleasing in his sight.

Scripture

I Corinthians 11:3, Ephesians 1:3, Psalm 107:42, Proverb 10:18

Prayer/thoughts:

In The Mixture of Mercy and Grace

Psalm 75

Choices have made life for some of us total chaos. Just because a thing looks good, sounds okay and makes us feel wonderful we accept it into our lives without even thinking twice about what God says about it. Our flesh can make us a *"right now"* kind of individual and we think we can handle the consequences after the fact. Truth is the same cup we continue to drink from for our good pleasure is the same cup we must drink from in our day of judgment. God holds such a cup; so, we might want to rethink this a bit.

Here is the content of this cup perhaps: wine (good to settle stomach), mixed with Galatians 5:17-21). You guessed it wine mixed with the lust of the flesh; the *"right nows"*. In this, you shall drink it all. There will be no escape for continuing in sin. But, God makes a way for us now to change this thing around. You will reap what you sow but there is a mixture to the wine.

God's mercy can go into the cup. His compassion and forgiveness towards us is his good pleasure to give. God's grace can also go into this cup. His presence with us is a must. To be in his presence and seeking forgiveness and turning makes the cup more delectable drink from than flesh. He holds this cup and no one else gets to stir but him. Power belongs to our God. In the mixture of mercy and grace is where we can find power.

Prayer

Father there is power in the name of your son Jesus. Fill my cup Lord and fill it up Lord. My soul is Lord is longing for your mercy and grace. By the hand of your Spirit fill me up and make me whole. Amen.

Declaration

I declare by the mercy and grace of God that the cup I shall drink will not be filled with self pleasures but the will of God.

Scripture

Galatians 5, Romans 7:18, Romans 12:2, I Corinthians 9:27

Prayer/thoughts:

Change of Heart Because of Prayer

"Confess your faults one to another, and pray one for another, that ye may be healed. The effectual fervent prayer of a righteous man availeth much."

James 5:16

rayer the language the opens up our communication and relationship to God is the one useful tool that never fails to aid us in our daily walk of life. Confession helps especially when a person is lying before God just as well of the other person. Having a relationship with a person of God is an awesome wonder because that relationship often times yields good results. This is not a flesh issue of intimacy, but one where one takes the time to pray with us and for us. We all have been asked if you communicate to our pastors what we are dealing with and going through, but, how often do we actual use a true person of God.

Hear closely what is being said in *". . . and pray one for another, that ye may be healed."* That should spark some godly relationships to share more in the word of God and prayer. This healing is not just for the body that may be ill but also for heart and mind to be healed. When prayer is done from the pureness of one's heart, much comes from it. Paul says that he also has to apply this same word of God to himself unless he too would be a castaway. This word is applicable to all that believe in the words of prayer and power of prayer. What an awesome tool we have with prayer.

There is a friend known from childhood and the confessions made between the two merited an hour or more of prayer. The results were phenomenal. Talk about a mighty change in both lives! The one knowing the words and power of prayer and the other learning prayer beyond one's self; now, that is a powerful ignition to bring God closer!

Prayer

Jesus, bring me closer through prayer. I want a change of heart to where I will confess and pray, Lord, not just for myself. I want to pray for those that would even honor me enough to speak to and pray with and for them. Deliver us all in Jesus name Amen.

Declaration

I declare that my prayers will be effectual and fervent and that in so being all will be healed.

Scripture

Mark 11:24, Galatians 5:22-23, James 1:5-8, I John 3:19-24

Prayer/thoughts:

Obedience to a Higher Authority

A higher authority has nothing to with titles when a choice is given to us as to whom we should listen to. It is an exact truth that every word that God has spoken since time began is right. To look at our creator and know he is our father is cause for obedience. He knows our ins and outs. He has place parents, preachers, teachers and employers before us that they may instruct us in some of our rights and from some of our wrongs. What is most intricately woven into every one of us is the one voice that we can't deny. What makes this voice so significant and distinguished is that even when we don't see him we hear him. There is something about when he calls us by name and speaks directly into us that we move. No other high ranking authority will ever get this kind of attention and obedience out of us. For certain, when God looks upon those he created; what he saw was that it was good. This obedience is good no matter what opposition tries to exert its authority over the author and the finisher of our lives.

Prayer

Most High God, I pray for obedience unto you, a most high obedience. I thank you for all those that walk in total obedience to your will and live according to your will in Jesus name. Amen

Declaration

I declare that I will obey you and your word for they are life even unto everlasting, for you are the Most High God.

Scriptures

John 10:27, I Samuel 15:22, Romans 13:1-5, I Peter 2:13-17, Ephesians 6:1

Prayer/thoughts:

Seeing the Best In Me

"But the Lord said unto Samuel, Look not on his countenance, or on the height of his stature; because I have refused him: for the Lord seeth not as man seeth; for man looketh on the outward appearance, but the Lord looked on the heart.

I Samuel 16:7

Perhaps when we look at God's creation of man, we find in Genesis that we are made in the likeness and image of him. We don't find him starting and stopping and doing over until disobedience was found in the hearts and minds of men. Can you find in God the emotion he felt in the making of man when man had fallen so deep into wickedness and perverted the whole earth? Out of an inhabited earth he saved one family.

It is for certain that most people have questioned why they exist. They are average, ordinary, everyday people. So, why am I here? It goes back to choice and the fact the God made us to be just like him. When he breathed life into the nostrils and man became a living soul, God put some gifts and talents within what he created. Notice, it comes from within. We look at backgrounds, neighborhoods, cultures, clothing, and smells and over all body structure. What has that to do with what he knows is there within. Right when we can't see anything; he sees the best. Why does he see the best? Could it be that it's because we are the likeness and image of him? There is potential to come forth and be all that we can be. That is the best in me and that's why I am still in existence.

Keyword: Potential

Prayer

Lord, I thank you for knowing what you have put in me and seeing my potential to allow me space and time to come forth of this potential. Amen

Declaration

I declare that I will seek and search for the best that has been put into me by God Almighty.

Prayer/thoughts:

Authentic Character

". . . ²⁷And he answering said, Thou shalt love the Lord thy God with all thy heart, and with all thy soul, and with all thy strength, and with all thy mind; and thy neighbor as thy self . . ."

Luke 10:25-37

Being genuine to who you know God has designed you to be is one of the most important things you can do. How often do you as man or woman of God mimic and mark the character of someone else because you believe it to enhance who you are? God created each person uniquely and wants us to perform life with vigor as we learn Him. The truth lies within you. Once you tap into this source of truth; love will reveal itself and you. This love will teach you just how to love with all of you; your heart, your soul, your strength, and your mind. It will make it so that you will want to show this to God in every component of your existence that He gave you this life and with this life you will show the living that was breathe into you by Him. This love is so unconditional that it will cause you to reach out beyond yourself to help a friend in need and be a friend indeed. This is one thing you know without a shadow of a doubt that you if you were in need would want and expect that same care. Be true to that love in you and show forth with all you have whom you love and know will bring all good to pass.

Prayer

In the name of Jesus, Lord I ask to come forth and show all the love you have shown to me to you in the things I do and to my neighbor whom I don't know but will know in character you have blessed me to have in you. Amen

Declaration

I declare that I will love the Lord with all my heart, soul, strength and mind and that I will love my neighbor even as I love myself in all that you have made me.

Scripture

Genesis 2:7, Mathew 7:12, James 5:16

Prayer/thoughts:

Non Burdensome Performance

"Then he answered and spake unto me, saying, This is the word of the Lord unto Zerubbabel, saying, Not by might, nor by power, but by my Spirit saith the Lord of host."

Zachariah 4:6

When you want to build up the kingdom of God, the first thing that comes to you is the flesh. What it can do and for how long. You will begin to worry and add stress and strain knowing how large the kingdom of God has appeared before you. You will automatically reach for a brother or a sister to help in your efforts to be an effective builder and it is not that you should look at being helpers one to another but, will you listen to what God is saying? When God is in the midst of the task at hand to build for Him; He will send a word to you so you will know exactly how His kingdom is to be built. Here is a simple warning: Physical might was not to build His kingdom, nor the loud and strong. He says to you to build up His kingdom it is by His Spirit. You must have His Spirit. You must go by His Spirit. It will be by His Spirit that He will send in according to His word and His purpose whom He wants building His kingdom. His Spirit will not burden the body, not the finance, or those that will come and go and do absolutely nothing to build His kingdom especially within you. He will by His Spirit build His kingdom in you and round about you.

Prayer

Lord, according to your Spirit build within and round about me your kingdom. It is your Spirit that will lead, guide and instruct by your word, for your yolk is easy, and your burden is light. Amen

Declaration

I declare that I will not go by power or by might but by Your Spirit in Jesus name.

Scriptures

Luke 22:42, John 14:16-17

Prayer/thoughts:

The Gifts Given

"Thus said the Lord, thy Redeemer, the Holy One of Israel; I am the Lord thy God which teacheth thee to profit, which leadeth thee by the way thou shouldest go."

Isaiah 48:15

Everything you will ever need God say "I AM." Often times you think of profit as money. Truth is, if you really had money what would you do with it. The profit that you have was given to you at the beginning when he spoke in the great and mighty power of his triune existence. He created a gift to himself that is in the likeness and the image of him both male and female. He breathed into you and your first very distinctive gift to profit with was you became a living soul. Not only that, but gave you dominion over everything around you he created. In the process, he teaches you how to stand, how to have peace, how to pray, how to serve, how to be loyal and dedicated. He has shown you how to follow after him. Further he has shown you a way of escape from the snares of the fowler. Look what you have; you have the Father, the Savior and Holy Ghost. That is only part of the gifts. What about the fruit you bare. This is what has been given in you from Elohim. Even in your nothing, you have something. Even in your sowing he gives you more seed that you may continue sowing. At the end of sowing you have a harvest. Gifts and more gifts you will have as long as you stay with the Great and Mighty Elohim.

Prayer

Father in the name of Jesus which you have given to me to profit through the Holy Ghost; I ask for my gifts to be manifest that I might profit your kingdom by that which you have given to me. Amen.

Declaration

I declare that every gift and every perfect gift that has been given to me will and shall be used to glorify and magnify the Lord.

Scriptures

Galatians 5:22-23, Isaiah 55:10, Genesis 1:26-28, Mathew 1:21, Acts 1:8

Prayer/thoughts:

Supply Is Complete

~*~

"But my God shall supply all your needs according to his riches in glory by Christ Jesus"

Philippians 4:19

~*~

Learning Jesus is something to be desired especially when you feel unequipped and knowing little or nothing about him. The easiest way to know him and his ways is to ask. While you are asking don't forget to mention that you need his Spirit in you and some understanding. Most times because you have not asked but assumed you have nothing. The other component is you ask amidst of what you truly need. Thank God for the Spirit that makes intercession for you with moans and groans that can't be uttered. Faith is a key that you must have.

I once told a friend that until you show God that you believe him for what she needed it would not be given to her. Needless to say after a year or so of learning to have faith and wait of Him; all of her needs started to manifest. Humble pie was being given to her and she didn't even know it. If you are prideful, you will always feel you can get it yourself and you are not going to ask anybody for anything. One of the names of God is El Shaddai which means *to overpower or to destroy*. It also means to *sustain or nurture*.

The God you serve will keep you, will destroy the enemy both inside and out of you. With El Shaddai present in your life everything you will ever need will be there for you richly. Just keep in mind this supply is what you need not what you want.

Prayer

Lord God, because you are a keeper and a destroyer of everything not good; give me what I need and destroy all that is about me that I don't need. In Jesus name Amen.

Declaration

I declare that El Shaddai will be my sustainer and my destroyer for my life.

Scriptures

Prayer/thoughts:

God Is Able and Provides

The God you serve has everything you need. In the midnight hour of distress and not knowing what to do or who to talk to; you will find that He is able to hear you as you speak and apply the answer that will comfort your mind. In other words He provides peace in the inward parts of you and calmness towards the outside of you. Have you ever been in a need of say $20 for gas to get to work and not have it when you first check your finance and all of a sudden being in the right place at the right time, around the right people and the right question comes as to "How are you doing? Is everything alright?" God provides the solution and the only thing you have to do at this point is state your case. There was once a person that was so lonely, so empty, so lost and alls he wanted was to see hope in his current over all being; no one could help him. But, one day he went to church service and the message of God came forth as Him being "Jehovah Jireh the Great Provider." By the time he left the service this man's whole demeanor changed. He was no longer empty or lonely. He felt peace. He realized that he actually had more than enough because he had the Great Provider with him. Allowing

God to speak to you and work for you; you will see just how able He is to provide every promise He has made to keep you sound.

Prayer

Father God you are more than enough for me. You able to provide the least and the greatest of my needs and I thank you and will trust in you forever. Amen

Declaration

I declare that from hence forth I will trust God for all my provisions both carnal and spiritual and proclaim him to be the God that will provide all my needs.

Scriptures

II Chronicles 25:9, Daniel 3:17, Mathews 10:28 Hebrews 5:7, Romans 14:4

Prayer/thoughts:

The Difference

Believe it or not, you make the difference when you allow yourself to see the blessings in the entire calamity that comes your way. Of course you will feel weak and in need. These needs that come are not always a tangible need but a need to lean and trust in Jesus. When you can say "But God" knowing He will supply all your needs according to His riches in glory. It seems that everything is falling down all around you, you make the difference when you express openly that your help comes from the Lord. Yes, people will come against you, but in all this will you be confident. You make the difference when you will not allow the enemy to tell you that you are nothing when God has made you something or when the enemy tells you that you don't have anything or ever will be anything; you will be able to know and say "I am because He is". The rudiments of this world may call you weak but when you stand in Christ and suffer all these things for His sake then you are strong and you make the difference.

Prayer

Jesus, thank you for making me strong for your sake even when everything around me would cause me to be weak; help me to make the difference by showing how great you are. Amen

Declaration

I declare that I am not weak, but strong in Jesus my Savior forever.

Scriptures

Romans 8:38, Philippians 4:13, Psalms 121:1-8

Prayer/thoughts:

Consequences When Praise Is in the Belly

"For his anger endureth but a moment; in his favor is life; weeping may endure for a night, but joy cometh in the morning."

Psalm 30:5

O ften we go through trials and tribulations. We cry and sob and even fret as long as we don't have an understanding as to where our help comes from in our crisis. He will not let the enemy triumph over us as long as we give all that we have over to him. Folks will laugh and talk about us and even look at us funny. But, because we are still present and here in the now God's favor is life. We may not have done things correctly and because of sin he has been angry with our dealings in life. However, to keep the enemy from advancing any further; we must praise. The question is how can we praise when everything and everyone around us says not so. In the inner part of us, this is in our belly, we find God still there saying press forward; even with darkness in our face. Lift Him up! The consequences of praise, brings light into dark sinful places. Sin and darkness cannot comprehend it and will flee. Praise will not come from the outer to bring joy and a new day. It is in our knowing whom we belong to in the first place that brings praise. Mornings of refreshing come when we acknowledge just how merciful he has been while we turned away from him to do our own thing. Praises going up bring blessings down in spite of us.

Prayer

Jesus, when we were yet sinners, you died for us. When we have come to acknowledge our sins before you Lord God, you have yet saved us. Thank you for favor and joy in knowing you as our savior. Amen

Declaration

I declare that I will not wait for sin to cause me to praise God Almighty, but I will praise him even in my darkest hour. For I know if I lift him up, he will refresh me in his time.

Scriptures

Psalm 103:8-9, Exodus 4:14, Deuteronomy 4:24

Prayer/thoughts:

He Is My Healer

"How God <u>anointed</u> Jesus of Nazareth <u>with</u> the Holy Ghost and <u>with</u> power; who went about doing good, and <u>healing all</u> that were oppressed of the devil; for God was with him."

Acts 10:38

For all the things that have plagued your mind and you didn't know how to have peach in your head it is because the enemy got a hold of your thoughts. Perhaps you chose to speak out aloud about the things that troubled you. Have you ever had a headache from thinking too much? Were the thoughts good for you and others about you or were they evil? God says he will keep you in perfect peace whose mind is stayed on him. Sickness can come because of something you've done or it can come as a test of faith. Often when illness is sudden or persistent the first thing you will do is seek over the counter remedies, next your call the physician's office or track yourself to the emergency room for relief; only to find another medicine that leaves traces behind called side effects. Did you pray first or seek God for help? Your help comes from above if you believe that. Sickness is not for the believer in Christ Jesus or for one who walks upright before the Lord. *Jehovah Rapha*, God the Healer or Great Physician of all time can take away all your sickness of the mind and the body. It takes deep rooted faith to get healed. This is not just for you but for whom you are willing to go to Jesus for to be healed as well. You have not because you ask a midst. Meaning, you are asking the wrong person. Learn his name, there is healing in the name of Jesus!

Prayer

Lord, thank you for anointing Jesus to heal me of all manner of sickness that is within me. It is you that made the body. You are the Word of life therefore I ask that my body obey the Word that I be healed completely in Jesus name. Amen

Declaration

I declare that by the power and anointing of Jesus Christ and the Holy Ghost that I shall be and I will be healed.

Scriptures

Exodus 15:26, Galatians 6:7–8

Prayer/thoughts:

Redeemed

To be called by name and able to respond by the meaning of who you are is wonderful. Even though DNA says who your biological parents are; God still has a way of defining just who you really are. Even coming from backgrounds not solid of much of anything but despair and oppression, God has called you by name and allowed you to know just how precious you are in His sight. Often you might feel as if you don't belong or have a family, but being called by name of Him means to be regarded as His. The fear you once felt if gone. The sense of knowing whose you really are opens up. You now know you can go through and He will not only guide you through but He will protect you and bring you out of all troubles. Even before you called out to be saved Jesus came for you. Redeemed properly means ransomed by means of a price. That price is Christ.

Prayer

Dear Lord Jesus, thank you for redeeming me by giving yourself ransom that I might know my name. Amen

Declaration

I declare that the redeemed I am called by my name and I belong to God.

Scriptures

I Peter 2:9-10, Revelation 5:9, Deuteronomy 13:5

Prayer/thoughts:

The Way to Results

"⁶Is not this the fast that I have chosen? to loose the bands of wickedness, to undo the heavy burdens, and to let the oppressed to free, and that ye break every yoke? . . . ¹²And they that shall be of thee shall build the old waste places: thou shalt raise up the foundations of many generations: and thou shalt be called, The repairer of the breach, The restorer of paths to dwell in."

Isaiah 58:6-12

In search of getting God's attention for most of what you desire to do for Him comes with the simple price of denying yourself the daily consumption of food and many other daily routines. Fasting in this sense is afflicting the body in order to get right through to the heart. You must empty out yourself if you expect God to move. You must afflict your soul that it cries out unto Him. His word will come to you but as you deny yourself you will find that the tempter will come also to block and distort your efforts. Prayer is a must and it has to be according to what His word says. This is not a time to be selfish. It is a time that He has chosen a fast that will undo the wrong all over. He says the fast He has chosen will loose, undo, free and break. The results: to build, to raise, and to be called! If you truly want to work for the Lord and bring in the lose to be saved; fast and seek the Lord. Inquire what He wants and how He wants it. Then, follow the path He gives.

Prayer

Father, just as you have said, I will not fast as I have, but that I will fast by your choice that the results will bring you glory in Jesus name. Amen

Declaration

I declare as I am lead by the power of God to fast and seek His face I will come forth to give Him glory.

Scriptures

Isaiah 58:6-12, Matthew 17:21

Prayer/thoughts:

My Help Cometh

~*~

"Let us therefore come boldly unto the throne of grace, that we may obtain mercy, and find grace to help in time of need.

Hebrew 4:16

~*~

There are many times when the enemy has come up against me to take all that God has given and sometimes it feels as if I could never make it especially on my own. Being one who only had to nod or make a call and things would happen quickly as far as help to get the enemies I encountered off me. Since learning Christ and all His righteousness, transition took place. My mind has been renewed and transformed. Now, I call on the Lord and His host to help me. Although I am certainly on the wall; I don't have to look back over my shoulder trying to see what's going on around me. One thing about it when God says He will help you and deliver you; He will do just that. Oh, to watch David hide within the cleft of the rocks while the enemy tracked all around about him; he waited and the God that is the same today, yesterday and forever more helped even to deliver the giant Goliath into Israel's hands by a rock and a sling shot can do the same for you now. Waiting on God is one of the biggest struggles you have next to believing. He will not let the enemy triumph over you He will come and e will not tarry!

Prayer

Lord thank you for being my very present help in the time of trouble. You always have the exact moment to move in my approaching unto you. Continue to bless me with the right boldness in my approach that you will bless me with the right help in Jesus name. Amen

Declaration

I declare that I will continue to learn the right boldness to approach my God at His throne to obtain help.

Scriptures

Psalm 121:2, Isaiah 41:10, 13, Psalm 46:1

Prayer/thoughts:

Perfect Peace

~*~

"Thou wilt keep him in perfect peace, whose mind is stayed on thee; because he trusteth in thee."

Isaiah 26:3

~*~

There are so many promises that God has given to His people. He has promised food, shelter and clothing. He has gone through great lengths to protect us from the fowler. So, when you are at such a busy time within your day or even your night, He can send a wave of peace over you. There had to be a peace He gave to Paul and Silas while locked up in prison. Have you ever taken time to notice the peace they held while being chained. Perfect peace will cause you to sing songs and pray prayers of faith. It will cause you to walk and take your time when usually you would be in a rush. Perfect peace will lower your voice yet speak with authority that will prove you out instead of you trying to prove yourself out. Whatever bondage you may be in, in your mind or your home perfect peace will guide you straight to the answer. Perfect peace my dear friend will let you sleep at night because you will have confidence in your keeper Jesus Christ. It is not in necessarily finding a quiet place but in finding a place within you to keep quiet and let it work on your behalf. In other words: have faith in knowing the God that said He will keep you. The only way to know Him is to seek Him and learn Him.

Prayer

Lord God you said I will be kept in perfect peace if I will keep my mind stayed on you. You are peace and you have spoken that peace would be still in my life. Thank you for perfect peace. Amen

Declaration

I declare the words spoken that peace will be perfect in my life according to Isaiah 26:3 and my faith in God to keep me.

Scriptures

Proverb 3:1-2, Luke 7:50, John 14:27, Hebrews 12:14

Prayer/thoughts:

No Way of Fainting

"I had fainted, unless I had believed to see the goodness of the Lord in the land of the living. Wait on the Lord; be of good courage, and he shall strengthen thine heart: wait, I say on the Lord."

Psalm 27:13-14

So many ups and downs and turn arounds in your life that you have not been able to see goodness anywhere tread? Most times it is because you have not truly looked for goodness. Goodness comes in the simplest and rarest forms. One of the first things God spoke of was "light". The Genesis tells us that God saw the light to be good and separated light from darkness. Light has been provided to the earth ever since. Genesis even goes on to say that God used the brighter light to rule the day and the lesser for the night. When day breaks within you what was there before? The sight you had prior was not quite light but a bit dim. When things don't happen right away; you become discouraged and start feeling misplace and you allow doubt to weaken you. You know, that's a part of fainting. If you could just wait on Him the goodness will begin to appear. By singing songs and making melody in your heart and reading the assurance of God's word while you wait is goodness. In fact, anything that you can think to do in the Spirit of God is good and it will not let you faint. It will strengthen you. That is called waiting. That is called believing that if you continue you will see the goodness of the Lord manifest itself right before you and in you. There is no way you can faint in the Lord God's goodness!

Prayer

God with your word you have upheld me. You have come in and changed me. When I look at how I waited in you I have to say thank you Lord as I wait do it again and again. Amen

Declaration

I declare that I will not and I shall not faint. I will and I shall see the goodness of the Lord. I will wait and I shall wait on the Lord.

Scriptures

Job 28:13, Psalm 142:5

Prayer/thoughts:

The Entrance of the King of Glory

Often in your times of seeking Christ the motion of the head is tilted downward. Understand there is humility and humbleness in you that causes this reaction when you are coming to Jesus, but after you have come and the search truly begins; the bowed down head is lifted up. The reason your head will lift up is because your eyes, your ears, your nose and your mouth can be noted as gates and doors for the entry of King Jesus to come in. He is not dead. He has risen; He is high and lifted up. Therefore upon reaching this level of finding Him, where He can enter in is through spiritual eyes, and ears, and nose and mouth. The whole entrance is upward. Your worship is often indicated with your hands lifted up and your eyes lifted and looking up and your voice lifted up. The more raised you are in the Spirit; the more the King of glory *shall come* in. He makes an entrance by the acknowledgement of who He is. The only way to do this is to hear the command that has been given to *lift up*! Then the word says *the King of glory shall come in!*

Prayer

Jesus you said if you be lifted up from the earth you would draw all men unto you. You said that you stand at the door and knock and if I harden not my heart you would come in and sup with me. My door is open; Lord, I invite you in that your glory will fill me through and through. Amen

Declaration

I declare to lift my head. I declare that my gates and my doors will be open unto you that your glory shall fill me through and through in Jesus name.

Scriptures

Psalm 121:1, John 12:32, Revelation 3:20

Prayer/thoughts:

Proving God

"Bring ye all the tithes into the storehouse, that there may be meat in mine house, and prove me now herewith, saith the Lord of hosts, if I will not open you up the windows of heaven, and pour you out a blessing, that there shall not be room enough to receive it."

Malachi 3:10

Here in this verse of God's word and even in this chapter of your life; God is giving a message and a promise and the part that many may not like is God also is giving a command concerning something that is thought to be in your possession. That is in most of today's terms, money. To take the first part of what you have and bring it to God constitutes four things that God says in this third chapter of Malachi: 1) Meat in God's house to carry on His work. 2) Opening of the windows of heaven to pour out a blessing so big there is no room. 3) Rebuking of the devourer so he will not destroy the source. 4) Recognition of God's blessings by all men. Simple, yet a struggle to bring all that tenth to Him and place it before Him for His work that He does daily, year in and year out. Proving that He is the source, and the God, of the whole earth who has all that is ever truly needed. Make this note: this is not a tempting but a proving of trust towards Him to make a provision, provide a way out of what He has asked for. There is a saying that; *you can't beat God's giving!* Even in the fourth mentioned thing, is found the testimony and blessings of those who will fall in according to the word.

Prayer

Father in the name of Jesus I come asking for the spirit of fear and selfishness to leave so that the giving to you may actually manifest itself in the midst of your people to your glory forever. Amen

Declaration

I declare that I will pay my tithe unto the Lord as proving He will do just what He said according to His word.

Scriptures

Luke 6:38, Proverb 3:9, II Corinthians 9:6-7, Matthew 25:29, James 1:17

Prayer/thoughts:

How Rivers Flow

"In the last day, that great day of the feast, Jesus stood and cried saying, If any man thirst, let him come unto me, and drink. He that believeth on me, as the scripture hath said, out of his belly shall flow rivers of living water."

John 7:37–38

Believing starts a move. As one would be thirsty for something to take away the dryness within the mouth or throat so is it in the spirit. Our spirit gets faint when it is not given encouragement to press on. When Jesus speaks to us through His word, He quenches by His Spirit all the fiery darts that have been lunged into us to create dryness. For some the loving care of being given the word of God has kept us from fainting and fading away. One thing about a river is it flows. It is not stale or stagnant. A moving river is alive. Life exists in flowing rivers. Life even comes to a flowing river to aid in it being refreshed and rejuvenated. Jesus is living water and He says if you thirst come and drink of me. He is living word. All that God speaks manifests itself. So, to believe the word of God means that life flows in the inward parts of the belly. If those that have come and drank and believe what they have taken in; when they speak the words that Christ has spoken to them; then out of their belly according to scripture/the word spoken "shall flow rivers of living water"! Make a note: this is Christ speaking to all both saved and unsaved shall receive the Spirit of truth flowing out if belief is in the belly.

Prayer

Father, your son Jesus said if I thirst to come and drink of him and if I believe as scripture has said that from my belly shall flow rivers of living water. I thirst and I believe. Be it so unto me in Jesus name. Amen

Declaration

I declare as I thirst after Christ and believe His word I shall flow with rivers of living water.

Scriptures

Matthew 3:11, Galatians 3:14, Luke 24:49, John 14:12

Prayer/thoughts:

A Name that Always Saves

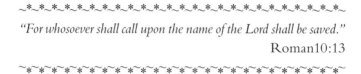

"For whosoever shall call upon the name of the Lord shall be saved."

Roman10:13

here is only one name throughout the Bible that has the power to save. No matter where this name is there is that kind of power. There is no name greater than the Lord Jesus Christ. In His name is healing. In His name is comfort. In His name is joy. If there is any name a man can give to another that would save them it would be *Jesus*. The heart of God towards man, created the image and the likeness of Him to redeem man; Christ to be our example. There is nothing that He has not gone through that He can't save. Look, in that name was sufferings, tempting as every point of man and He is the only one that kept His original design in image and likeness without sin. The perfect man that could transcend time from beginning to the end, He has been there and is here and will be forever more. He knows, He cares, He hears and He shares. If the desire is to come out of perplexity, call Jesus He will satisfy. He can raise the dead, heal the sick and can feed a multitude just by speaking a word. Jesus is the only one who can stand between God and man and present man to be accepted by the Father. Establish a relationship that will allow the saving use of His name in your life so that you can *go and sin no more*.

Prayer

Father, there is power in the name of your only begotten Son. Establish me in the name of Jesus that I will be saved always o matter the circumstance. Amen.

Declaration

I declare to call upon the name of Jesus which saves to the utmost corners of the earth. For I declare that there is power in the name of Jesus.

Scriptures

Matthews 1:21, Proverb 18:10, Acts 4:12

Prayer/thoughts

Dressed to Stand

~*~

"Wherefore <u>take unto you</u> the whole armour of God, <u>that</u> ye may be able to withstand in the evil day, and having done all, to stand."

Ephesians 6:13

~*~

As Christians the question has been what to wear. However, being clothed in righteousness is far greater an effect than the style and fashion for going to church and being seen of men. There are so many obstacles that take our attention away to the matters at hand that we truly should be prepped for. To be concerned with who will have something to say or not has nothing to do with the salvation being snatched away because we are dressed improperly to stand and guard what God has so graciously given. God says to take to you the whole armour of Himself, that you may be able to withstand all the violent changes in your time and knowing what to do with what you have. By the fourteenth verse of Ephesians chapter six a descriptive adage is mention of what to take on to you to be dressed. Notice that instead of what you were subject to put on, God informs in commands and promises. Get ready because there is a battle and to come through and still exist at what comes at you, you will need some "up-top" and "front-gear" to stand firmly. Look how solid this armour can get based on faith and trust in the word carried from within. Are you dressed to stand?

Prayer

Father in the name of Jesus I come to you asking to be equipped and dressed in your truth about life that I will have the ability to stand. Amen

Declaration

I declare to put on and to wear the armour my Lord and Savior has given to me to stand in the evil day until He comes.

Scriptures

Ephesians 6:10-18, Colossians 3:22-25, I Thessalonians 5:8, Isaiah 59:17, Romans 6:12, Matthews 4:4-11, II Corinthians 10:4-6

Prayer/thoughts:

Where Grace Appeared

~*~

"For the grace of God that bringeth salvation hath appeared to all men. Teaching us that, denying ungodliness and worldly lusts, we should live soberly, righteously, and godly, in this present world; Looking for that blessed hope, and the glorious appearing of the great God and our Saviour Jesus Christ:"

Titus 2:11-13

~*~

It is great the blessings of grace have appeared to us and will appear again. What grace brings is salvation. It just didn't appear to a select few but all men. Grace teaches to deny ungodliness, worldly lusts and further to live soberly, righteously, godly in this life that is before all men right now. Grace also teaches to look for the rapture and the coming of Christ again. There is no way and no excuse that none should perish. Opportunity is now, to live and learn how God wants His people. Yes, you can live this life just as described in the text. The foundation has been laid and the way opened up to as many as would receive, believe, accept and do according to His will. There is an age old song with words that say; "the angels are beckoning me from heavens golden doors." As you journey on up-hill to the Lord doesn't something within say "let me show you the way". The way Christ has gone is the way that must be mimicked. His life was exemplified by having a mind and a heart to do the will of His heavenly Father. Don't you want to see Him?

Prayer

In the name of Jesus, Lord I come asking you to show me the way I am to live. I look to go away some day and I want to deny myself all that is not like you for that day.

Declaration

I declare that as the Lord shows me that I will deny all that is in me to follow Him more and more and more that grace may teach me in Jesus name.

Scriptures

Ephesians 2:8-9, John 3:16, Revelations 22:17, Titus 2:2-7, Hebrews 12:14, Romans 8:12-13, Philippians 3:20, II Timothy 3:12

Prayer/thoughts:

A Shift

"And be not conformed to this world: but be ye transformed by the renewing of your mind, the ye may prove what is that good, and acceptable, and perfect, will of God."

Romans 12:2

You can't give in to everything around you the way it has been set and altered to go against what God has actually said to do, to live, to be, to go and to come. If you take time to notice conformity really sets back and holds, and hinders progress that is to come about. Paul states in Hebrews six chapter "let us press on to perfection." You can no longer sit still knowing that God has brought you out of conformity to show forth His praise by the expression of faith you have as you think on Him daily. There is a part of you that renews with every passing moment of life that is experienced in Christ that you must unleash. As transformation takes place, a shift positions you into the proving of what is good and acceptable and perfect will of God for not just you but all that is around you. There are benefits in these kinds of shifts. So transform as you learn Him. There is no way you can ever have an old mind again going in accordance with renewal daily.

Prayer

Lord in the name of Jesus I come asking for a shift change in my mind towards doing what is good and acceptable in your sight. Amen

Declaration

I declare in the precious blood of Jesus as my mind is cleansed from the conformity of this world that I be changed to prove the good, the acceptable and perfect will of God.

Scriptures

Matthews 17:2, II Corinthians 3:18, Titus 3:5, II Corinthians 4:16, Colossians 3:10, Ephesians 4:23

Prayer/thoughts:

Time

"To every thing there is a season and a time for every purpose under the heaven:"

Ecclesiastes 3:1

~*~

Who would have thought that last year at this time you would be a search for inner strength and searching the word of God to dig deeper into yourself to find His purpose in you. It is a time and season for knowledge of what your purpose truly is in God. How much time will you put into your purpose that it will be fulfilled? Have you set the clock for your devotional time with God and His word? What is the season calling for? What areas is God showing you to work in? Your purpose and the purpose God has for you in whatever season you are in He gives time to it all that you may work it out until the next season comes. Within this season make sure that you have dedicated time to prayer and study into that area. Meditate on the word and just spend time with God so that it will strengthen you as you move forward. Make declarations according to the word you believe and watch God show you where you have come from to where you are now. Time will show. Keep a journal as you go so you can see your growth of strength for the times and seasons of your life in Christ.

Prayer

Father I come to you in the name of Jesus asking you to strengthen as I progress forward in you. I thank you for the casting off and the pulling down, for the building up and the increase that you have done in me. My life is in your hands.

Declaration

I declare that I will walk out every season and purpose given to me in time with what God wants me to be.

Scriptures

Genesis 18:14, Hebrews 9:27, Matthews 15:13, John 10:10, James 4:7-10, II Timothy1:14, Psalm 2:4, I Corinthians 13, Romans 5

Prayer/thoughts:

Some More Scriptures On Strength

Philippians 4:13—I can do all things through Christ which strengtheneth me.

Deuteronomy 31:6—Be strong and of a good courage, fear not, nor be afraid of them: for the LORD thy God, he it is that doth go with thee; he will not fail thee, nor forsake thee.

Deuteronomy 20:4—For the LORD your God is he that goeth with you, to fight for you against your enemies, to save you.

1 Corinthians 10:13—There hath no temptation taken you but such as is common to man: but God is faithful, who will not suffer you to be tempted above that ye are able; but will with the temptation also make a way to escape, that ye may be able to bear it.

Isaiah 41:10—Fear thou not; for I am with thee: be not dismayed; for I am thy God: I will strengthen thee; yea, I will help thee; yea, I will uphold thee with the right hand of my righteousness.

2 Corinthians 12:9-10—And he said unto me, My grace is sufficient for thee: for my strength is made perfect in weakness. Most gladly therefore will I rather glory in my infirmities, that the power of Christ may rest upon me.

Matthew 11:28—Come unto me, all ye that labour and are heavy laden, and I will give you rest.

Psalms 39:7—And now, Lord, what wait I for? my hope is in thee.

Matthew 6:33—But seek ye first the kingdom of God, and his righteousness; and all these things shall be added unto you.

Psalms 31:24—Be of good courage, and he shall strengthen your heart, all ye that hope in the LORD.

Ecclesiastes 4:9-13—Two [are] better than one; because they have a good reward for their labour.

Isaiah 40:31—But they that wait upon the LORD shall renew their strength; they shall mount up with wings as eagles; they shall run, and not be weary; and they shall walk, and not faint.

1 Corinthians 16:13—Watch ye, stand fast in the faith, quit you like men, be strong.

Romans 8:28—And we know that all things work together for good to them that love God, to them who are the called according to his purpose.

James 5:16—Confess [your] faults one to another, and pray one for another, that ye may be healed. The effectual fervent prayer of a righteous man availeth much.

1 Corinthians 6:19-20—What? know ye not that your body is the temple of the Holy Ghost which is in you, which ye have of God, and ye are not your own?

1 Timothy 5:8—But if any provide not for his own, and specially for those of his own house, he hath denied the faith, and is worse than an infidel.

Romans 8:1—There is therefore now no condemnation to them which are in Christ Jesus, who walk not after the flesh, but after the Spirit.

Psalms 41:3—The LORD will strengthen him upon the bed of languishing: thou wilt make all his bed in his sickness.

Exodus 15:2—The LORD is my strength and song, and he is become my salvation: he is my God, and I will prepare him an habitation; my father's God, and I will exalt him.

Philippians 2:13—For it is God which worketh in you both to will and to do of his good pleasure.

Nahum 1:7—The LORD is good, a strong hold in the day of trouble; and he knoweth them that trust in him.

Isaiah 12:2—Behold, God is my salvation; I will trust, and not be afraid: for the LORD JEHOVAH is my strength and my song; he also is become my salvation.

Hebrews 3:1-19—Wherefore, holy brethren, partakers of the heavenly calling, consider the Apostle and High Priest of our profession, Christ Jesus;

Nehemiah 8:10—Then he said unto them, Go your way, eat the fat, and drink the sweet, and send portions unto them for whom nothing is prepared: for this day is]holy unto our Lord: neither be ye sorry; for the joy of the LORD is your strength.

Mark 12:30—And thou shalt love the Lord thy God with all thy heart, and with all thy soul, and with all thy mind, and with all thy strength: this [is] the first commandment.

Daniel 10:19—And said, O man greatly beloved, fear not: peace be unto thee, be strong, yea, be strong. And when he had spoken unto me, I was strengthened, and said, Let my lord speak; for thou hast strengthened me.

Isaiah 40:21-30—Have ye not known? have ye not heard? hath it not been told you from the beginning? have ye not understood from the foundations of the earth?

Isaiah 40:1-31—Comfort ye, comfort ye my people, saith your God.

Psalms 66:1-20—Make a joyful noise unto God, all ye lands:

Job 12:16—With him is strength and wisdom: the deceived and the deceiver are his.

1 Peter 4:11—If any man speak, let him speak as the oracles of God; if any man minister, let him do it as of the ability which God giveth: that God in all things may be glorified through Jesus Christ, to whom be praise and dominion for ever and ever. Amen.

Jeremiah 1:18—For, behold, I have made thee this day a defenced city, and an iron pillar, and brasen walls against the whole land, against the kings of Judah, against the princes thereof, against the priests thereof, and against the people of the land.

Proverbs 4:18—But the path of the just is as the shining light, that shineth more and more unto the perfect day.

Joshua 1:9—Have not I commanded thee? Be strong and of a good courage; be not afraid, neither be thou dismayed: for the LORD thy God is with thee whithersoever thou goest.

Revelation 7:12—Saying, Amen: Blessing, and glory, and wisdom, and thanksgiving, and honour, and power, and might, be unto our God for ever and ever. Amen.

Hebrews 6:18—That by two immutable things, in which it was impossible for God to lie, we might have a strong consolation, who have fled for refuge to lay hold upon the hope set before us:

Philippians 1:28—And in nothing terrified by your adversaries: which is to them an evident token of perdition, but to you of salvation, and that of God.

Ephesians 1:19—And what is the exceeding greatness of his power to us-ward who believe, according to the working of his mighty power,

1 Corinthians 1:8—Who shall also confirm you unto the end, that ye may be blameless in the day of our Lord Jesus Christ.

Acts 3:7—And he took him by the right hand, and lifted [him] up: and immediately his feet and ankle bones received strength.

John 5:9—And immediately the man was made whole, and took up his bed, and walked: and on the same day was the sabbath.

Zechariah 1:18—Then lifted I up mine eyes, and saw, and behold four horns.

Habakkuk 1:11—Then shall his mind change, and he shall pass over, and offend, imputing this his power unto his god.

Jeremiah 9:23—Thus saith the LORD, Let not the wise [man] glory in his wisdom, neither let the mighty man glory in his might, let not the rich man glory in his riches:

Psalms 23:1-4—The LORD is my shepherd; I shall not want.

Nehemiah 1:10—Now these are thy servants and thy people, whom thou hast redeemed by thy great power, and by thy strong hand.

2 Kings 18:20—Thou sayest, but they are but vain words, I have counsel and strength for the war. Now on whom dost thou trust, that thou rebellest against me?

1 Samuel 2:9—He will keep the feet of his saints, and the wicked shall be silent in darkness; for by strength shall no man prevail.

1 Samuel 2:4—The bows of the mighty men are broken, and they that stumbled are girded with strength.

Exodus 13:14—And it shall be when thy son asketh thee in time to come, saying, What is this? that thou shalt say unto him, By strength of hand the LORD brought us out from Egypt, from the house of bondage:

Hebrews 13:4—Marriage is honourable in all, and the bed undefiled: but whoremongers and adulterers God will judge.

Ephesians 6:10—Finally, my brethren, be strong in the Lord, and in the power of his might.

Romans 5:6—For when we were yet without strength, in due time Christ died for the ungodly.

Acts 13:1-3—Now there were in the church that was at Antioch certain prophets and teachers; as Barnabas, and Simeon that was called Niger, and Lucius of Cyrene, and Manaen, which had been brought up with Herod the tetrarch, and Saul.

John 5:8—Jesus saith unto him, Rise, take up thy bed, and walk.

Luke 10:19—Behold, I give unto you power to tread on serpents and scorpions, and over all the power of the enemy: and nothing shall by any means hurt you.

Matthew 26:52-54—Then said Jesus unto him, Put up again thy sword into his place: for all they that take the sword shall perish with the sword.

Habakkuk 3:16-19—When I heard, my belly trembled; my lips quivered at the voice: rottenness entered into my bones, and I trembled in myself, that I might rest in the day of trouble: when he cometh up unto the people, he will invade them with his troops.

Nahum 1:12—Thus saith the LORD; Though they be quiet, and likewise many, yet thus shall they be cut down, when he shall pass through. Though I have afflicted thee, I will afflict thee no more.

Lamentations 1:6—And from the daughter of Zion all her beauty is departed: her princes are become like harts that find no pasture, and they are gone without strength before the pursuer.

Jeremiah 17:5—Thus saith the LORD; Cursed be the man that trusteth in man, and maketh flesh his arm, and whose heart departeth from the LORD.

Jeremiah 12:5—If thou hast run with the footmen, and they have wearied thee, then how canst thou contend with horses? and [if] in the land of peace, wherein thou trustedst, they wearied thee, then how wilt thou do in the swelling of Jordan?

Isaiah 43:1-28—But now thus saith the LORD that created thee, O Jacob, and he that formed thee, O Israel, Fear not: for I have redeemed thee, I have called thee by thy name; thou art mine.

Proverbs 21:22—A wise man scaleth the city of the mighty, and casteth down the strength of the confidence thereof.

Psalms 46:1—God is our refuge and strength, a very present help in trouble.

Psalms 18:1 I will love thee, O LORD, my strength.

1 Samuel 2:10—The adversaries of the LORD shall be broken to pieces; out of heaven shall he thunder upon them: the LORD shall judge the ends of the earth; and he shall give strength unto his king, and exalt the horn of his anointed.

Judges 16:17—That he told her all his heart, and said unto her, There hath not come a razor upon mine head; for I [have been] a Nazarite unto God from my mother's womb: if I be shaven, then my strength will go from me, and I shall become weak, and be like any other man.

Genesis 2:24—Therefore shall a man leave his father and his mother, and shall cleave unto his wife: and they shall be one flesh.

Revelation 12:10—And I heard a loud voice saying in heaven, Now is come salvation, and strength, and the kingdom of our God, and the power of his Christ: for the accuser of our brethren is cast down, which accused them before our God day and night.

Revelation 1:16—And he had in his right hand seven stars: and out of his mouth went a sharp twoedged sword: and his countenance was as the sun shineth in his strength.

2 Peter 3:18—But grow in grace, and in the knowledge of our Lord and Saviour Jesus Christ. To him be glory both now and for ever. Amen.

James 1:27—Pure religion and undefiled before God and the Father is this, To visit the fatherless and widows in their affliction, and to keep himself unspotted from the world.

1 Timothy 1:12—And I thank Christ Jesus our Lord, who hath enabled me, for that he counted me faithful, putting me into the ministry;

2 Corinthians 12:9—And he said unto me, My grace is sufficient for thee: for my strength is made perfect in weakness. Most gladly therefore will I rather glory in my infirmities, that the power of Christ may rest upon me.

Acts 9:19—And when he had received meat, he was strengthened. Then was Saul certain days with the disciples which were at Damascus.

Acts 6:8—And Stephen, full of faith and power, did great wonders and miracles among the people.

John 18:1-40—When Jesus had spoken these words, he went forth with his disciples over the brook Cedron, where was a garden, into the which he entered, and his disciples.

John 5:11—He answered them, He that made me whole, the same said unto me, Take up thy bed, and walk.

Luke 10:27—And he answering said, Thou shalt love the Lord thy God with all thy heart, and with all thy soul, and with all thy strength, and with all thy mind; and thy neighbour as thyself.

Luke 1:51—He hath shewed strength with his arm; he hath scattered the proud in the imagination of their hearts.

Matthew 5:13—Ye are the salt of the earth: but if the salt have lost his savour, wherewith shall it be salted? it is thenceforth good for nothing, but to be cast out, and to be trodden under foot of men.

Matthew 5:1-48—And seeing the multitudes, he went up into a mountain: and when he was set, his disciples came unto him:

Hosea 7:9—Strangers have devoured his strength, and he knoweth it not: yea, gray hairs are here and there upon him, yet he knoweth not.

Daniel 11:15—So the king of the north shall come, and cast up a mount, and take the most fenced cities: and the arms of the south shall not withstand, neither his chosen people, neither shall there be any strength to withstand.

Daniel 10:18—Then there came again and touched me one like the appearance of a man, and he strengthened me,

Daniel 10:16—And, behold, one like the similitude of the sons of men touched my lips: then I opened my mouth, and spake, and said unto him that stood before me, O my lord, by the vision my sorrows are turned upon me, and I have retained no strength.

Lamentations 1:14—The yoke of my transgressions is bound by his hand: they are wreathed, [and] come up upon my neck: he hath made my strength to fall, the Lord hath delivered me into their hands, from whom I am not able to rise up.

Lamentations 1:11—All her people sigh, they seek bread; they have given their pleasant things for meat to relieve the soul: see, O LORD, and consider; for I am become vile.

Isaiah 10:13—For he saith, By the strength of my hand I have done it, and by my wisdom; for I am prudent: and I have removed the bounds of the people, and have robbed their treasures, and I have put down the inhabitants like a valiant man:

Isaiah 1:1-31—The vision of Isaiah the son of Amoz, which he saw concerning Judah and Jerusalem in the days of Uzziah, Jotham, Ahaz, and Hezekiah, kings of Judah.

Proverbs 8:14—Counsel is mine, and sound wisdom: I am understanding; I have strength.

Psalms 81:1—Sing aloud unto God our strength: make a joyful noise unto the God of Jacob.

Psalms 27:1—The LORD is my light and my salvation; whom shall I fear? the LORD is the strength of my life; of whom shall I be afraid?

Psalms 19:14—Let the words of my mouth, and the meditation of my heart, be acceptable in thy sight, O LORD, my strength, and my redeemer.

Psalms 18:2—The LORD is my rock, and my fortress, and my deliverer; my God, my strength, in whom I will trust; my buckler, and the horn of my salvation, and my high tower.

Job 21:23—One dieth in his full strength, being wholly at ease and quiet.

Job 12:13—With him is wisdom and strength, he hath counsel and understanding.

Job 2:13—So they sat down with him upon the ground seven days and seven nights, and none spake a word unto him: for they saw that his grief was very great.

Some Scriptures on Love

Deuteronomy 6:5—And thou shalt love the LORD thy God with all thine heart, and with all thy soul, and with all thy might.

1 Corinthians 13:4-13—Charity suffereth long, and is kind; charity envieth not; charity vaunteth not itself, is not puffed up,

Matthew 22:37-39—Jesus said unto him, Thou shalt love the Lord thy God with all thy heart, and with all thy soul, and with all thy mind.

1 Corinthians 16:14—Let all your things be done with charity.

1 John 4:8—He that loveth not knoweth not God; for God is love.

Leviticus 19:18—Thou shalt not avenge, nor bear any grudge against the children of thy people, but thou shalt love thy neighbour as thyself: I am the LORD.

2 Chronicles 15:13—That whosoever would not seek the LORD God of Israel should be put to death, whether small or great, whether man or woman.

1 John 4:19—We love him, because he first loved us.

1 John 4:12—No man hath seen God at any time. If we love one another, God dwelleth in us, and his love is perfected in us.

1 John 4:18—There is no fear in love; but perfect love casteth out fear: because fear hath torment. He that feareth is not made perfect in love.

Mark 12:30—And thou shalt love the Lord thy God with all thy heart, and with all thy soul, and with all thy mind, and with all thy strength: this is the first commandment.

Galatians 5:22—But the fruit of the Spirit is love, joy, peace, longsuffering, gentleness, goodness, faith,

1 Corinthians 13:13—And now abideth faith, hope, charity, these three; but the greatest of these is charity.

John 14:15—If ye love me, keep my commandments.

1 Corinthians 13:1-13—Though I speak with the tongues of men and of angels, and have not charity, I am become a sounding brass, or a tinkling cymbal.

1 Timothy 1:5—Now the end of the commandment is charity out of a pure heart, and of a good conscience, and of faith unfeigned:

1 Corinthians 13:8—Charity never faileth: but whether there be prophecies, they shall fail; whether there be tongues, they shall cease; whether there be knowledge, it shall vanish away.

John 3:16—For God so loved the world, that he gave his only begotten Son, that whosoever believeth in him should not perish, but have everlasting life.

1 Peter 4:8—And above all things have fervent charity among yourselves: for charity shall cover the multitude of sins.

Romans 8:38-39—For I am persuaded, that neither death, nor life, nor angels, nor principalities, nor powers, nor things present, nor things to come,

1 Peter 2:17—Honour all men. Love the brotherhood. Fear God. Honour the king.

1 John 4:7—Beloved, let us love one another: for love is of God; and every one that loveth is born of God, and knoweth God.

Philippians 1:9—And this I pray, that your love may abound yet more and more in knowledge and in all judgment;

Ephesians 4:32—And be ye kind one to another, tenderhearted, forgiving one another, even as God for Christ's sake hath forgiven you.

Ephesians 6:24—Grace be with all them that love our Lord Jesus Christ in sincerity. Amen.

1 John 2:15—Love not the world, neither the things that are in the world. If any man love the world, the love of the Father is not in him.

1 Thessalonians 5:11—Wherefore comfort yourselves together, and edify one another, even as also ye do.

Matthew 22:37—Jesus said unto him, Thou shalt love the Lord thy God with all thy heart, and with all thy soul, and with all thy mind.

Matthew 19:19—Honour thy father and [thy] mother: and, Thou shalt love thy neighbour as thyself.

John 15:13—Greater love hath no man than this, that a man lay down his life for his friends.

1 Timothy 6:10—For the love of money is the root of all evil: which while some coveted after, they have erred from the faith, and pierced themselves through with many sorrows.

1 John 4:21—And this commandment have we from him, That he who loveth God love his brother also.

John 15:12—This is my commandment, That ye love one another, as I have loved you.

1 Thessalonians 3:12—And the Lord make you to increase and abound in love one toward another, and toward all men, even as we do toward you:

1 John 3:18—My little children, let us not love in word, neither in tongue; but in deed and in truth.

Revelation 3:19—As many as I love, I rebuke and chasten: be zealous therefore, and repent.

2 Timothy 2:22—Flee also youthful lusts: but follow righteousness, faith, charity, peace, with them that call on the Lord out of a pure heart.

Matthew 5:44-45—But I say unto you, Love your enemies, bless them that curse you, do good to them that hate you, and pray for them which despitefully use you, and persecute you;

1 Peter 3:9—Not rendering evil for evil, or railing for railing: but contrariwise blessing; knowing that ye are thereunto called, that ye should inherit a blessing.

John 15:9-17—As the Father hath loved me, so have I loved you: continue ye in my love.

1 John 4:11—Beloved, if God so loved us, we ought also to love one another.

1 Timothy 6:2—And they that have believing masters, let them not despise them, because they are brethren; but rather do them service, because they are faithful and beloved, partakers of the benefit. These things teach and exhort.

Matthew 25:34-40—Then shall the King say unto them on his right hand, Come, ye blessed of my Father, inherit the kingdom prepared for you from the foundation of the world:

Matthew 10:42—And whosoever shall give to drink unto one of these little ones a cup of cold water only in the name of a disciple, verily I say unto you, he shall in no wise lose his reward.

Mark 9:41—For whosoever shall give you a cup of water to drink in my name, because ye belong to Christ, verily I say unto you, he shall not lose his reward.

Matthew 10:41—He that receiveth a prophet in the name of a prophet shall receive a prophet's reward; and he that receiveth a righteous man in the name of a righteous man shall receive a righteous man's reward.

Galatians 5:14—For all the law is fulfilled in one word, even in this; Thou shalt love thy neighbour as thyself.

Romans 13:8-10—Owe no man any thing, but to love one another: for he that loveth another hath fulfilled the law.

Mark 12:29-31—And Jesus answered him, The first of all the commandments is, Hear, O Israel; The Lord our God is one Lord:

Psalms 23:1-6—The LORD [is] my shepherd; I shall not want.

Romans 12:10—Be kindly affectioned one to another with brotherly love; in honour preferring one another;

Ruth 1:16-17—And Ruth said, Intreat me not to leave thee, or to return from following after thee: for whither thou goest, I will go; and where thou lodgest, I will lodge: thy people shall be my people, and thy God my God:

Philippians 2:2—Fulfil ye my joy, that ye be likeminded, having the same love, being of one accord, of one mind.

Galatians 5:26—Let us not be desirous of vain glory, provoking one another, envying one another.

Galatians 5:22-23—But the fruit of the Spirit is love, joy, peace, longsuffering, gentleness, goodness, faith,

Mark 12:31—And the second is like, namely this, Thou shalt love thy neighbour as thyself. There is none other commandment greater than these.

Psalms 27:7—Hear, O LORD, when I cry with my voice: have mercy also upon me, and answer me.

1 John 5:2—By this we know that we love the children of God, when we love God, and keep his commandments.

1 John 2:9-11—He that saith he is in the light, and hateth his brother, is in darkness even until now.

Galatians 6:10—As we have therefore opportunity, let us do good unto all [men], especially unto them who are of the household of faith.

Romans 14:19—Let us therefore follow after the things which make for peace, and things wherewith one may edify another.

Ephesians 3:17-19—That Christ may dwell in your hearts by faith; that ye, being rooted and grounded in love,

Romans 15:7—Wherefore receive ye one another, as Christ also received us to the glory of God.

John 15:17—These things I command you, that ye love one another.

Luke 10:1-27—After these things the Lord appointed other seventy also, and sent them two and two before his face into every city and place, whither he himself would come.

Song of Solomon 8:6-7—Set me as a seal upon thine heart, as a seal upon thine arm: for love is strong as death; jealousy is cruel as the grave: the coals thereof are coals of fire, which hath a most vehement flame.

1 John 3:11—For this is the message that ye heard from the beginning, that we should love one another.

1 John 2:5—But whoso keepeth his word, in him verily is the love of God perfected: hereby know we that we are in him.

1 Peter 1:8—Whom having not seen, ye love; in whom, though now ye see him not, yet believing, ye rejoice with joy unspeakable and full of glory:

Galatians 4:20—I desire to be present with you now, and to change my voice; for I stand in doubt of you.

1 Corinthians 13:4—Charity suffereth long, [and] is kind; charity envieth not; charity vaunteth not itself, is not puffed up,

John 13:34—A new commandment I give unto you, That ye love one another; as I have loved you, that ye also love one another.

Isaiah 1:1-31—The vision of Isaiah the son of Amoz, which he saw concerning Judah and Jerusalem in the days of Uzziah, Jotham, Ahaz, and Hezekiah, kings of Judah.

Jude 1:21—Keep yourselves in the love of God, looking for the mercy of our Lord Jesus Christ unto eternal life.

1 John 5:3—For this is the love of God, that we keep his commandments: and his commandments are not grievous.

1 John 4:7-16—Beloved, let us love one another: for love is of God; and every one that loveth is born of God, and knoweth God.

1 John 3:23—And this is his commandment, That we should believe on the name of his Son Jesus Christ, and love one another, as he gave us commandment.

1 John 3:17—But whoso hath this world's good, and seeth his brother have need, and shutteth up his bowels of compassion from him, how dwelleth the love of God in him?

1 John 3:16-19—Hereby perceive we the love of God, because he laid down his life for us: and we ought to lay down our lives for the brethren.

1 John 3:16—Hereby perceive we the love of God, because he laid down his life for us: and we ought to lay down our lives for the brethren.

1 Peter 3:8—Finally, be ye all of one mind, having compassion one of another, love as brethren, be pitiful, be courteous:

Hebrews 6:10—For God is not unrighteous to forget your work and labour of love, which ye have shewed toward his name, in that ye have ministered to the saints, and do minister.

2 Timothy 1:4—Greatly desiring to see thee, being mindful of thy tears, that I may be filled with joy;

Colossians 2:1—For I would that ye knew what great conflict I have for you, and for them at Laodicea, and for as many as have not seen my face in the flesh;

1 Corinthians 13:4-8—Charity suffereth long, and is kind; charity envieth not; charity vaunteth not itself, is not puffed up,

John 3:16-17—For God so loved the world, that he gave his only begotten Son, that whosoever believeth in him should not perish, but have everlasting life.

Luke 10:27-30—And he answering said, Thou shalt love the Lord thy God with all thy heart, and with all thy soul, and with all thy strength, and with all thy mind; and thy neighbour as thyself.

Matthew 5:3-10—Blessed are the poor in spirit: for theirs is the kingdom of heaven.

Psalms 127:1-26—Except the LORD build the house, they labour in vain that build it: except the LORD keep the city, the watchman waketh but in vain.

Psalms 1:1-6—Blessed is the man that walketh not in the counsel of the ungodly, nor standeth in the way of sinners, nor sitteth in the seat of the scornful.

Joshua 1:9—Have not I commanded thee? Be strong and of a good courage; be not afraid, neither be thou dismayed: for the LORD thy God is with thee whithersoever thou goest.

Revelation 2:4—Nevertheless I have somewhat against thee, because thou hast left thy first love.

2 John 1:6—And this is love, that we walk after his commandments. This is the commandment, That, as ye have heard from the beginning, ye should walk in it.

1 John 5:1—Whosoever believeth that Jesus is the Christ is born of God: and every one that loveth him that begat loveth him also that is begotten of him.

1 John 3:14—We know that we have passed from death unto life, because we love the brethren. He that loveth not his brother abideth in death.

James 2:8—If ye fulfil the royal law according to the scripture, Thou shalt love thy neighbour as thyself, ye do well:

James 1:27—Pure religion and undefiled before God and the Father is this, To visit the fatherless and widows in their affliction, and to keep himself unspotted from the world.

James 1:12—Blessed is the man that endureth temptation: for when he is tried, he shall receive the crown of life, which the Lord hath promised to them that love him.

Hebrews 10:24—And let us consider one another to provoke unto love and to good works:

Some More Scriptures on Faith

Proverbs 3:5—Trust in the LORD with all thine heart; and lean not unto thine own understanding.

Ephesians 2:8—For by grace are ye saved through faith; and that not of yourselves: it is the gift of God:

2 Corinthians 5:7—For we walk by faith, not by sight:

Hebrews 11:6—But without faith it is impossible to please him: for he that cometh to God must believe that he is, and that he is a rewarder of them that diligently seek him.

1 John 5:4—For whatsoever is born of God overcometh the world: and this is the victory that overcometh the world, even our faith.

Mark 9:23—Jesus said unto him, If thou canst believe, all things [are] possible to him that believeth.

Luke 17:6—And the Lord said, If ye had faith as a grain of mustard seed, ye might say unto this sycamine tree, Be thou plucked up by the root, and be thou planted in the sea; and it should obey you.

Hebrews 11:1-39—Now faith is the substance of things hoped for, the evidence of things not seen.

Matthew 9:22—But Jesus turned him about, and when he saw her, he said, Daughter, be of good comfort; thy faith hath made thee whole. And the woman was made whole from that hour.

1 John 5:14—And this is the confidence that we have in him, that, if we ask any thing according to his will, he heareth us:

Philippians 4:13—I can do all things through Christ which strengtheneth me.

Ephesians 2:8-9—For by grace are ye saved through faith; and that not of yourselves: it is the gift of God:

Hebrews 11:1—Now faith is the substance of things hoped for, the evidence of things not seen.

Psalms 40:4—Blessed is that man that maketh the LORD his trust, and respecteth not the proud, nor such as turn aside to lies.

James 1:3—Knowing this, that the trying of your faith worketh patience.

Luke 7:50—And he said to the woman, Thy faith hath saved thee; go in peace.

Mark 11:23—For verily I say unto you, That whosoever shall say unto this mountain, Be thou removed, and be thou cast into the sea; and shall not doubt in his heart, but shall believe that those things which he saith shall come to pass; he shall have whatsoever he saith.

Matthew 9:29—Then touched he their eyes, saying, According to your faith be it unto you.

Mark 9:24—And straightway the father of the child cried out, and said with tears, Lord, I believe; help thou mine unbelief.

James 2:24—Ye see then how that by works a man is justified, and not by faith only.

Hebrews 13:5—Let your conversation be without covetousness; and be content with such things as ye have: for he hath said, I will never leave thee, nor forsake thee.

John 3:36—He that believeth on the Son hath everlasting life: and he that believeth not the Son shall not see life; but the wrath of God abideth on him.

1 Timothy 4:10—For therefore we both labour and suffer reproach, because we trust in the living God, who is the Saviour of all men, specially of those that believe.

Mark 11:22-24—And Jesus answering saith unto them, Have faith in God.

Acts 26:18—To open their eyes, and to turn them from darkness to light, and from the power of Satan unto God, that they may receive forgiveness of sins, and inheritance among them which are sanctified by faith that is in me.

Mark 5:25-34—And a certain woman, which had an issue of blood twelve years,

Hebrews 13:6—So that we may boldly say, The Lord is my helper, and I will not fear what man shall do unto me.

2 Timothy 1:12—For the which cause I also suffer these things: nevertheless I am not ashamed: for I know whom I have believed, and am persuaded that he is able to keep that which I have committed unto him against that day.

Acts 3:16—And his name through faith in his name hath made this man strong, whom ye see and know: yea, the faith which is by him hath given him this perfect soundness in the presence of you all.

James 1:12—Blessed is the man that endureth temptation: for when he is tried, he shall receive the crown of life, which the Lord hath promised to them that love him.

1 Peter 1:7—That the trial of your faith, being much more precious than of gold that perisheth, though it be tried with fire, might be found unto praise and honour and glory at the appearing of Jesus Christ:

Ephesians 6:16—Above all, taking the shield of faith, wherewith ye shall be able to quench all the fiery darts of the wicked.

Galatians 5:22—But the fruit of the Spirit is love, joy, peace, longsuffering, gentleness, goodness, faith,

Romans 8:28—And we know that all things work together for good to them that love God, to them who are the called according to his purpose.

Matthew 8:2—And, behold, there came a leper and worshipped him, saying, Lord, if thou wilt, thou canst make me clean.

1 Corinthians 2:5—That your faith should not stand in the wisdom of men, but in the power of God.

John 6:69—And we believe and are sure that thou art that Christ, the Son of the living God.

John 3:16—For God so loved the world, that he gave his only begotten Son, that whosoever believeth in him should not perish, but have everlasting life.

Psalms 18:6—In my distress I called upon the LORD, and cried unto my God: he heard my voice out of his temple, and my cry came before him, [even] into his ears.

Romans 15:13—Now the God of hope fill you with all joy and peace in believing, that ye may abound in hope, through the power of the Holy Ghost.

Luke 5:5—And Simon answering said unto him, Master, we have toiled all the night, and have taken nothing: nevertheless at thy word I will let down the net.

Matthew 9:21—For she said within herself, If I may but touch his garment, I shall be whole.

Isaiah 40:31—But they that wait upon the LORD shall renew their strength; they shall mount up with wings as eagles; they shall run, and not be weary; and they shall walk, and not faint.

Matthew 9:18—While he spake these things unto them, behold, there came a certain ruler, and worshipped him, saying, My daughter is even now dead: but come and lay thy hand upon her, and she shall live.

1 Samuel 14:6—And Jonathan said to the young man that bare his armour, Come, and let us go over unto the garrison of these uncircumcised: it may be that the LORD will work for us: for [there is] no restraint to the LORD to save by many or by few.

Galatians 3:1-29—O foolish Galatians, who hath bewitched you, that ye should not obey the truth, before whose eyes Jesus Christ hath been evidently set forth, crucified among you?

Romans 3:22-28—Even the righteousness of God which is by faith of Jesus Christ unto all and upon all them that believe: for there is no difference:

John 6:68—Then Simon Peter answered him, Lord, to whom shall we go? thou hast the words of eternal life.

Habakkuk 2:4—Behold, his soul which is lifted up is not upright in him: but the just shall live by his faith.

Isaiah 55:11—So shall my word be that goeth forth out of my mouth: it shall not return unto me void, but it shall accomplish that which I please, and it shall prosper in the thing whereto I sent it.

Hebrews 11:4—By faith Abel offered unto God a more excellent sacrifice than Cain, by which he obtained witness that he was righteous, God testifying of his gifts: and by it he being dead yet speaketh.

Ephesians 6:10-18—Finally, my brethren, be strong in the Lord, and in the power of his might.

John 20:31—But these are written, that ye might believe that Jesus is the Christ, the Son of God; and that believing ye might have life through his name.

Matthew 17:20—And Jesus said unto them, Because of your unbelief: for verily I say unto you, If ye have faith as a grain of mustard seed, ye shall say unto this mountain, Remove hence to yonder place; and it shall remove; and nothing shall be impossible unto you.

Genesis 50:20—But as for you, ye thought evil against me; but God meant it unto good, to bring to pass, as it is this day, to save much people alive.

Hebrews 6:13-15—For when God made promise to Abraham, because he could swear by no greater, he sware by himself,

Colossians 2:7—Rooted and built up in him, and stablished in the faith, as ye have been taught, abounding therein with thanksgiving.

Philippians 1:27—Only let your conversation be as it becometh the gospel of Christ: that whether I come and see you, or else be absent, I may hear of your affairs, that ye stand fast in one spirit, with one mind striving together for the faith of the gospel;

1 Samuel 17:37—David said moreover, The LORD that delivered me out of the paw of the lion, and out of the paw of the bear, he will deliver me out of the hand of this Philistine. And Saul said unto David, Go, and the LORD be with thee.

Revelation 3:20—Behold, I stand at the door, and knock: if any man hear my voice, and open the door, I will come in to him, and will sup with him, and he with me.

Revelation 2:19—I know thy works, and charity, and service, and faith, and thy patience, and thy works; and the last to be more than the first.

Hebrews 11:24-28—By faith Moses, when he was come to years, refused to be called the son of Pharaoh's daughter;

Hebrews 10:39—But we are not of them who draw back unto perdition; but of them that believe to the saving of the soul.

Hebrews 10:35—Cast not away therefore your confidence, which hath great recompence of reward.

Galatians 2:16—Knowing that a man is not justified by the works of the law, but by the faith of Jesus Christ, even we have believed in Jesus Christ, that we might be justified by the faith of Christ, and not by the works of the law: for by the works of the law shall no flesh be justified.

Romans 8:39—Nor height, nor depth, nor any other creature, shall be able to separate us from the love of God, which is in Christ Jesus our Lord.

Romans 8:37—Nay, in all these things we are more than conquerors through him that loved us.

Romans 8:35—Who shall separate us from the love of Christ? shall tribulation, or distress, or persecution, or famine, or nakedness, or peril, or sword?

Psalms 7:1—O LORD my God, in thee do I put my trust: save me from all them that persecute me, and deliver me:

2 Kings 18:5—He trusted in the LORD God of Israel; so that after him was none like him among all the kings of Judah, nor any that were before him.

2 Peter 3:13—Nevertheless we, according to his promise, look for new heavens and a new earth, wherein dwelleth righteousness.

James 1:6—But let him ask in faith, nothing wavering. For he that wavereth is like a wave of the sea driven with the wind and tossed.

Hebrews 13:7—Remember them which have the rule over you, who have spoken unto you the word of God: whose faith follow, considering the end of their conversation.

Hebrews 11:7—By faith Noah, being warned of God of things not seen as yet, moved with fear, prepared an ark to the saving of his house; by the which he condemned the world, and became heir of the righteousness which is by faith.

Hebrews 10:38—Now the just shall live by faith: but if any man draw back, my soul shall have no pleasure in him.

Hebrews 6:12—That ye be not slothful, but followers of them who through faith and patience inherit the promises.

2 Timothy 4:7—I have fought a good fight, I have finished my course, I have kept the faith:

1 Timothy 1:19—Holding faith, and a good conscience; which some having put away concerning faith have made shipwreck:

2 Thessalonians 1:3-5—We are bound to thank God always for you, brethren, as it is meet, because that your faith groweth exceedingly, and the charity of every one of you all toward each other aboundeth;

Romans 10:6-10—But the righteousness which is of faith speaketh on this wise, Say not in thine heart, Who shall ascend into heaven? that is, to bring Christ down from above:

Mark 16:16—He that believeth and is baptized shall be saved; but he that believeth not shall be damned.

Matthew 13:58—And he did not many mighty works there because of their unbelief.

Matthew 9:28—And when he was come into the house, the blind men came to him: and Jesus saith unto them, Believe ye that I am able to do this? They said unto him, Yea, Lord.

2 Chronicles 32:7—Be strong and courageous, be not afraid nor dismayed for the king of Assyria, nor for all the multitude that is with him: for there be more with us than with him:

Hebrews 12:2—Looking unto Jesus the author and finisher of our faith; who for the joy that was set before him endured the cross, despising the shame, and is set down at the right hand of the throne of God.

Hebrews 11:32—And what shall I more say? for the time would fail me to tell of Gedeon, and of Barak, and of Samson, and of Jephthae; of David also, and Samuel, and of the prophets:

Hebrews 11:16-39—But now they desire a better country, that is, an heavenly: wherefore God is not ashamed to be called their God: for he hath prepared for them a city.

2 Timothy 2:11-13—It is a faithful saying: For if we be dead with him, we shall also live with him:

2 Timothy 1:13—Hold fast the form of sound words, which thou hast heard of me, in faith and love which is in Christ Jesus.

1 Timothy 3:9—Holding the mystery of the faith in a pure conscience.

Colossians 1:23—If ye continue in the faith grounded and settled, and [be] not moved away from the hope of the gospel, which ye have heard, and which was preached to every creature which is under heaven; whereof I Paul am made a minister;

Galatians 5:6—For in Jesus Christ neither circumcision availeth any thing, nor uncircumcision; but faith which worketh by love.

2 Corinthians 4:16-18—For which cause we faint not; but though our outward man perish, yet the inward man is renewed day by day.

Romans 10:17—So then faith cometh by hearing, and hearing by the word of God.

Romans 3:23—For all have sinned, and come short of the glory of God;

2 Chronicles 32:8—With him is an arm of flesh; but with us is the LORD our God to help us, and to fight our battles. And the people rested themselves upon the words of Hezekiah king of Judah.

Jude 1:21—Keep yourselves in the love of God, looking for the mercy of our Lord Jesus Christ unto eternal life.

1 Peter 1:21—Who by him do believe in God, that raised him up from the dead, and gave him glory; that your faith and hope might be in God.

1 Peter 1:8—Whom having not seen, ye love; in whom, though now ye see him not, yet believing, ye rejoice with joy unspeakable and full of glory:

Hebrews 11:23—By faith Moses, when he was born, was hid three months of his parents, because they saw he was a proper child; and they were not afraid of the king's commandment.